I0455005

Eyes

Within

John Sieren as told to Vye Sieren Carlile

Dedicated to our mother, Mary Helen Sieren, who was always so very supportive of any of our endeavors! Here's to you, Mom!

Eyes

Within

A laid back and from the heart look at how a young man destined for nowhere, according to his high school counselor, surmounted all obstacles and became educated and employed!

John Sieren as told to Vye Sieren Carlile

Masabi Publications

PO Box 2663
Salem, OR 97308
www.masabi.org

©2012 by John Sieren and Vye Carlile. All rights reserved.

No part of this book may be reproduced, stored in a retrieval system, or transmited by any manner without the written permission of the author.

Published by Create Space.

ISBN 13 978-1479133253
ISBN 10 1479133256

The views expressed in this work are solely those of the author and do not necessarily reflect the views of the publisher and the publisher hereby disclaims any responsibility for them.

A compelling story of a young penitentiary guard and his insightful and totally delightful experiences

Eyes Within

By John as told to his oldest sister, Vye, who had to have literary freedom to add to things to make 'em just right....So, John's story is partly true and partly, well, partly, fiction.... You know these smart-alec sisters who think they know everything and screw up everything you have ever told them? Well, these things could have happened, be they to John or some other poor sucker who thought he could enter the halls of jurisprudence and create civility. So, on with the story!

Fall, 2005, the date Vye started writing the story, not the date John started the action in the story....

Chapter One
The Beginning of an Adult Life

It was my first day working at the penitentiary. I had always wanted to be a cop. Ever since I was a little boy. I think it was the uniform. My dad was in the Army and wore uniforms to work. They looked sharp and impressive. After my brief stint in the Army, I still wanted that look. Working for the penal system would work out nicely for me, I thought.

But back to that first day....

I had no clue where to go. I was in the penitentiary. I was in that uniform. I had a gun, but I couldn't wear it in the yard. I had a stick and a whistle, but I didn't know what to do. No one gave me explicit orders. I sort of stood there like a deer in the headlights. Then I heard a gruff voice, "Sieren? That your name? Go out in the yard and watch the inmates there." And I did. That voice of power came not from my supervisor, but rather from one of the inmates!

I went out into the yard and just stood there. There were hundreds of men just lolly-gagging about. They all got real quiet and stared at me. I tried to look tough. I tried to emanate power. I was scared to death.

Most of the men returned to what they were doing. Some were walking and talking and others were throwing basketballs. Lots of cement. Lots of it. I kept thinking, "Man, if someone were to throw me down, that'd hurt like hell." Standing there thinking I must have been crazy to actually want to do this job, a guy came up behind me.

"You new here?"

"Yeah," I confessed.

"Don't worry. We're alright. Just treat us right and you won't have any problems.   Stand closer to the inmates and don't go into long diatribes – talk short. That works best. Just say 'what's up?'"

I wondered what the hell he was in prison for. He looked like he could have been a dentist or a lawyer, or something, but not an inmate. I wanted to ask him, but I wasn't ready to hear something horrible or despicable. I looked at him and he guessed what I was thinking.

"I'm what they call a white-collar inmate. I guess I didn't do my books just right. I should have known better. But I've learned a lesson. I keep learning it. When I get out, I'm gonna work with my brother and we're gonna have this accounting firm. Until then, if you need any help, just let me know."

Ole' Tom walked off with a swagger. Now was my turn to decide if he was on the level or not. Another more experienced officer finally made his way out to the yard.

"Well, Sieren, I guess you are gonna be baptized by fire rather than by water, eh?"

I had no clue what the hell he was talking about, but I was soon to find out.

Further out near the fence, I heard some loud talking. Nah, it wasn't talking. It was swearing and verbal abuse going on. I closed my eyes, took a deep breath, and looked again. The verbiage was slowly, but surely, turning into a nice physical treat for all the inmates as they gathered about.

The officer blew his whistle. I looked for mine, wondered if I should blow mine as well, and followed my mentor to the fence. The inmates parted as the Sea of Galilee must have. Two inmates were swearing and punching each other over a goddamned basketball. Was this fucking kindergarten? Jesus. What did I get myself into?

The officer shouted something about "Wanna go in the poky alone for a month this time? Move away and shut the hell up." I started to move away and then realized he was talking to the two jazzed up fighters. One threw the basketball and I was ready to call a foul when my fellow officer blew the whistle and told everyone to get back to what they were doing. The show was over.

Hum. Where was his pistol? His gun? His stuff? Then I realized that the guys in the yard don't have weapons. Hope the inmates didn't know that....

The other officer motioned for me to follow him. He pushed some lever and a loud friggin' blasting sound made me wanna fall flat on my face, 'cause there was nowhere in that yard to hide. It was simply the signal for the men to line up and go back inside. Sort of reminded me of school. Except not high school. More like grade school.

Teacher, do I look ok? Teacher, I need to piss. Teacher, I need to breathe. Teacher, I don't feel well. As each inmate passed, they had some damned sort of excuse for not going to work. I could have earned a teaching certificate and listened to this drivel.

All clear. All were in. Judging by the green in my face, the officer decided I needed a break. It had been 45 minutes since I arrived and I was already given a break. I squinted my eyes as I entered back into the dungeon. A long hall led to a break room for EMPLOYEES ONLY. How the hell would a visitor or an inmate get to this room? Why would they even want to?

I sat down and swore under my breath. Shit. I'm tired, hot, and hungry. It's only 3:45 pm. I had seven hours and fifteen minutes left to work. School hadn't prepared me for this rigor.... I laughed. School. I wasn't much of a student when I was younger.

Chapter Two
My Background

The counselor at my high school threatened all my teachers that if they didn't pass me as a senior, I'd be in their rooms the next year. I was 6'5" and weighed about 285 pounds. The football coach lusted for my skills. He even called my mom and promised to tutor me in exchange for my brawn on the field.

Mom was overprotective and did the best she could. That was to protect her only son. I may have had asthma, but it was from the damned Camel cigarette smoke drifting throughout the house. It got me out of a lot of work, but in the end I regretted not bucking her on these decisions not to let me be physical. Teachers were tired of my "kiss my ass" attitude and low scores.

Hell, they all passed me. Thanks to the counselor. I graduated from high school with my class with very little effort, I might add. Not that I'm proud of it, but it's fact. I didn't care much for book learning and still don't. Give me a ball. Give me a comfy lounger and a big screen TV with a remote. Give me a phone with unlimited minutes. Let me buy someone something and I'm fine.

It wasn't that I was a bad-ass. It was just that I was the youngest of three children, the two oldest being GIRLS. Being the only son and grandson for almost ten years gave me certain privileges, sort of God-like privileges my sisters might add.

I was the passer of the name. The connector of generations. I didn't have to clean up, iron, do dishes, or vacuum. That was girls' work and I was glad I wasn't one. The girls did the work. Mom did the cooking and Dad just sat around in his wife-beater t-shirt drinking coffee and chain-smoking his Camels. Occasionally, he'd bring home some putrid canned crap from the base and he'd heat it up, add in some beans and announce the chili was ready.

Or for Thanksgiving, he'd cut up a zillion onions, celery stalks, and bacon and add a little liquid and bread and announce the Army's best dressing was ready for the turkey. He didn't do things in small ways. We could eat out of the chili pot for a week and the dressing was enough to feed the entire neighborhood.

But they didn't come over. Mom didn't like strangers in the house. Pop, - well, he swore so bad we just thought it was ordinary speech. He didn't even know he swore after a while. They were just sounds. Sounds my oldest sister thought were German words until she went to college....

I hung out with a few friends, but that always got me into trouble. Teenage boys get very bored and when boredom hits, the shit can hit the fan. And so it did as a few of my buddies (each about a foot shorter than me) and I sat on a curb breaking Coke bottles.

A young cop pulled up and asked us what the hell we were doing.

Eyes Within

"Nothing," we said as we slammed another greenish tinted bottle on the curb. It made a wonderful sound and shards of glass slivers just went everywhere. If you could catch the sun right, they were like diamonds glittering on the hot paved streets.

"Boys, go home," the cop ordered, but pointed a finger at me, "except for you."

What the hell? What did I do? I only got to break one bottle. The others had the idea. Why was he picking on me?

He chewed a toothpick as he gazed at me.

"Uh, how old are you, son?" he politely inquired.

"Thirteen," I said. It was the truth. I was a big kid. But I didn't have an adult mind. I was just a kid.

I could tell by the look on his face that he didn't believe me. "Um," he repeated, "where do you live?"

"Just down the street," I pointed. If I squinted I could see our ranch style house with gray stone and a white rose trellis out front. My old man was in the garage tinkering with his tools and Mom was probably in the house cleaning the ceiling or some other place.

I thought maybe he would just let me walk down the street. Not on your life.

"Get in, kid," he demanded.

"Shit, the folks are gonna get pissed at me and I didn't do nothing," I wailed in my head. To the cop, I said, "Sir, I didn't do anything more than the others."

He was silent. I could tell he thought I was the perpetrator of the malicious play of little boys. Surely, because I didn't look like a little kid.

As we coasted down the street, the cop stopped and the old man looked out from the garage. He squinted and then said, "Goddamn it! What the hell have you done?" I gingerly stepped out of the patrol car.

Mom heard everything. If I coughed, she would come to see what the matter was. She ran outside, screaming, "Oh, God, what's the matter? What have you done? What's going on? What's wrong?"

Shut up. I thought. Just shut up. I haven't done a thing.

"Well, Ma'am, I was just bringing your son down to see how old he is."

Mom replied, "Well, he's thirteen."

"Damn!" laughed the cop. "He is a big-un. I thought he was seventeen if he was a day."

Then he told the saga of the stupid coke bottles and left, with nary an apology. What would the neighbors think? Jesus.

When I entered high school I adapted a thick skin on the outside so no damned cop or no damned teacher would ever make me feel like a fucking idiot again. I wasn't too bad, but I wasn't good either.

So, that ole' counselor told me that I better go in the Army. I wasn't smart enough to go to college. Hum, I guess he knew better than me. So I tried to go into the Army. Shit, no one told me that the Army was hard. No one told me that you didn't get much sleep, you didn't get to dress nice, nor did you get to eat what you wanted. Fuck that shit. I'm out of here. I lost a lot of weight and learned a lot of good lessons. Many a day I regretted the time I got out of the military. But destiny has our plans already made....

I called my Mom. Dad had already died. Mom was alone. Good thing. Now I could claim hardship. Get me out of this fuckin' place. I ain't gonna do this. It's way too hard.

Calisthenics, my ass. I lost forty pounds in a month and was way too hungry to do those rope a dope things. Nah, I was getting out. I wasn't suited for the Army. Maybe I could sell clothes. I always liked nice clothes.

Well, life on the outside wasn't much easier than the Army. Mom had found her a new love and moved herself on to California. I tried following a friend from school to Colorado, where I froze my ass off and tried to make a living on minimum wage jobs selling clothing. My car was a piece of shit, given that I had totaled the folks' red Torino.

Eyes Within

Pop had covered for me and I didn't get in trouble. I had been sixteen and had been drinking and couldn't see the damned road. When I woke up in the ditch on base, I walked until someone spotted me.

The officer recognized me as Pop's son (Pop had worked at a gas station to make ends meet) and let me go. I don't think those things happen today....

Colorado was too damned cold and too far away from family. Mom's new husband called me and said to get my ass down to California. I didn't have to be asked twice. A warm condo, food from my Mom and, hell, I could do what I want then. California, here I come....

I wasn't exactly prepared to work in my mid-twenties. I could sell clothes and I could complain loud and clear. Hum. What to do. I met a girl the opposite of my mom. Plain, maybe even dowdy. She didn't wear makeup, fix her hair high, or wear fancy clothing. That's it. I'll marry her. I bet she'll treat me right. She can cook and do all that girl stuff. I'll watch football and live life in the manner to which I was destined.

Eyes Within

Chapter Three
Job Quest

Now for a job. I was stressed that I didn't have a job wearing a uniform. I didn't want those low-entry jobs where you had to kiss someone's ass for forty years until you were promoted. I wanted power and I did think I wanted to make a difference.

I read somewhere they needed correctional officers. In the beginning, when I decided to join Law Enforcement, I chose the Department of Corrections. Why in the hell would I choose a career, where my life would be in danger and could end as fast as it started -- that's a hell of a job.

I found out that the California State Prisons were hiring. Actually, they were hiring anyone - blind, crippled or crazy, 21-81 years old, or it seemed.

 Boy, were they ever hiring!! This was in part due to the mass influx of "Gang Bangers" and all other serious criminals, "First Offenders" or not. The heyday of the golden age of the Twentieth Century Revolution all over again.

No, not the Industrial Revolution where the construction of cars and making things better for Americans was beginning, but this time the changes in the Criminal Justice System and the influx of new inmates and the new prisons coming on line, (opening) dictated a need for more employees.

I thought I may have found my life's work. I decided to put together a resume' and forward it to the Department of Corrections' Personnel Office. The process was long and tedious as I began my transition from ordinary citizen to officer in the prison.

I applied for "The Toughest Beat in the State" and waited ninety days to take a written test. Was it the pay? You bet! The chance for advancement and so on made me decide to apply to begin my career in the Department of Corrections.

I always enjoyed ride-alongs with cop friends in the past.It was exciting and was rewarding. It was never dull and always kept me on my toes and I always wanted to continue my interrupted army career in a paramilitary system.

My neighbor worked for the system and showed me his check and I thought, that's not much -- then he said, "That's my overtime."

God, I thought, it's more than my regular salary!! He gave me the short version of the responsibility of an officer and comparative salary of the ten "Highest paid Departments in the State" and I duly replied, "Where do I sign up?"

I did wonder if it was the respect, helping others, or saving the public from the "Gangsters" that swayed my decision,-- not—it was the "pay."

Yep, good old-fashion greed prevailed. The pay as a production controller in my current field would take several promotions and pay-raises to equal the starting pay and overtime that the state was offering. I soon found out that the process was tedious and took a lot of time, almost a year from start to the beginning of the Academy.

I repeat, the process was long and tedious as I began the process of joining up in the supposed toughest beat in the state. I guess some folks would have just given up and gone their merry way.

Why did I keep on waiting? For a better life. For the American dream. And, lastly, for some reason I wanted fulfillment in a job. Imagine that – wanting to be fulfilled in your daily life!

I decided I would drive to Folsom State Prison to see how long it would take me to get there. As I pulled up to the facility, I thought it looked more like a drab, smelly ole' dungeon. I was not impressed. How in the heck did I think I could make a difference here?

The prison had huge imposing iron gates and a stone fence as high as the eye could see and I felt a bit eerie approaching the façade. Did I really think I could work in a place like this?

It looked medieval to say the least. I was looking long and hard for the moat. How in the heck did I think I was going to make a difference in this system I continually asked myself.

First lesson in the correction's system was that I was glad I wasn't wearing any of the gang colors. Not that I knew ahead of time that might be a problem.

As I entered the building, I was informed of the rules of the area:
- Don't talk to the inmates in the area.
- Don't give the inmates anything.

- Don't take anything from them.

I strolled over to the arts and crafts area where various items were made and sold by inmates. Man, leather purses, art deco, no knives that I could see, but lots of cool things one might see at a Saturday flea market or even better.

I thumbed through some of the canvassed art and found one that really caught my eye. I knew the wife would love it as well.

"Hey, can you hold this for me until I leave?" I asked the person at the desk.

"Sure, I'm not going anywhere for twenty years," he guffawed.

Duh. He was an inmate. He didn't look like one. He didn't act like one. Boy, was I getting confused.

I had to do my business there – I mean, I wasn't there to shop. Which I liked. But nevertheless, I was there on business. I did my business. By this time I was more interested in returning to the shop and scrounging around for gifts than I was being tested to see if I could work here.

Returning to the desk, I paid for the purchase wondering who the artist was. What was he thinking when he painted? The landscape was so serene and well-developed.

Eyes Within

I could almost feel myself drifting into the painting and laying on a blanket, sipping some coke and watching the world go by....

The dreaded test. Something I had never actually excelled in – testing. I had nothing to study, no books or advice, so I decided to wing it. What else could I do? I returned to the center the following week. I had been told if you really want to do something, you can do it. Yeah, right, I thought.

On the way to take test, I almost got a speeding ticket. The California sun shone brightly and the heat hit the pavement and so did I. Maybe a bit too fast.

A highway cop was behind me with his lights and siren on. My heart began to pound so loud I could barely hear the siren. Thump, thump, thump. The police car passed me and kept on a goin'. Whew.

A ticket on the way to becoming part of law enforcement surely wouldn't look good. Someone was looking out for me. 'Cause the cop was on a mission and I weren't it! ☺

 Now all the demons that had possessed me all my life reared their ugly heads. *You can't do it. You aren't smart enough. You couldn't even stay in the army. You can't can't can't can't....*

I consoled myself that at least I still had my federal job. I could always turn back. Maybe it's curiosity just like passing a bad accident – you really don't want to look, but you do. You just gotta do it!

That close encounter with the law increased my stress level about seven hundred percent. As I entered the hallowed hall of the dreaded test, I could not believe the number of people there. It was filled to capacity. I thought that maybe I should just leave right then and there and avoid the rush at the end.

Oh, oh! They were passing out the booklets already and telling everyone to keep them closed. The proctor welcomed all of us and I began to freeze as I sat in my Bermuda shorts right under an AC vent. I have no clue what the guy talked about, other than I was freezing my ass off, I was stressed about the "almost" ticket, and I was damned hungry.

My stomach rumbled and my brain said, "RUN! QUICK!"

Just then my book was put in front of me. What's this? A damned dissertation? For a damned guard job? I thought that maybe I could excuse myself to the latrine and exit from there. I had no confidence. I started the test. I was even worried that I would misspell my own name. God! Are you there?

I wrote. I have no clue what. But I wrote. Then I got up to leave. My knees cracked as I got up half-glued to the chair. The upper part of my legs were frozen and the part stuck to the chair was glued with sweat that poured from the small of my back down my shorts and to the seat.

No kidding. I almost thought I had peed in my pants. But it was sweat. True. Just sweat.

We were told that the results would be posted in three to four weeks. Great. Now everyone would know how dumb I am.

Posted for all to see. John – no pass. When I returned to see the results I could not believe I had actually passed and with a whopping 94%. Hell, a 94 might have once been my temperature, but never a grade....What was going on here? Was God listening?

Chapter 4
Physical Training

Phase One Physical – The only exercise I was used to was running to the fast food places and munching down all those calories.

If you call shopping at the mall speed walking, then I was used to exercise. But now we were talking about EXERCISE. Not the natural movements of the body, but stuff that'd separate the wheat from the chaff. I think I was still the chaff...

The prison was beginning to look like home. Gray, stone, dark, depressing, and filled with people who'd rather not be there.

"Hey, I'm here to take a test for to be a guard," I laughed as I pulled up to the guard shack.

"Well, you follow that there yellow line to the white building. Then you go in and look for the personnel room. I am sure it's got a sign on the door. Have a nice day!" the guard drawled.

I passed the iron gate and went to the first cream colored building. I was redirected back to the front gate where I was supposed to be processed in. What a mess! I'm not looking for three hots and a cot. I am just here for a physical....

There were several of us and we huddled together as we approached the hospital area. I took a battery of physical agility tests and broke three machines. They were testing my physical and motor strength. They had the nerve to ask me not to break any more machines.

Eyes Within

A cute young candy striper came up to check my heart rate and all the men in the area, including me, had elevated heart rates.

Someone shouted, "Zip up your top! That's causing all the problems." An older, wider gal came by and took our heart rates and they were normal. It was the winter of '84 and I was on my way to report for training.

Eyes Within

Chapter 5
The Academy

I was accepted into the academy. Our class was small. There were thirty-nine of us total. Other classes had been near a hundred. We were a close class and our eight weeks of training seemed like years at times.

When it came time to find out who was accepted, I thought that if they called out your name, you were selected. I almost cried like a damned baby when I didn't hear my name, but then realized that was the roll call of those not selected for the academy. I was in.

But then hadn't I made a passing grade on the written test? Oh, this was the physical part....

Now that I was a member of the eight-week wonder team, I had to leave the wife and home and stay in the dorms at the academy. Of course, most of us left on the weekend to retreat into the warmth and safety of our own homes. I didn't need to travel far. Just to veg out and watch TV and eat and relax. That was the life....Except for the studying.

You can't just forget about your work life on the weekends. You gotta figure out how to stay afloat and not flunk out! Lots of people did – in our small group only two washed out.

I was determined to make it come hell or high water. So for one of the few times in my life, I sat down and made myself study. A lot of what we learned was damned common sense.

I got that from Pop. He had a lot of common sense and very little formal education. My friend Anthony helped me a lot, too.

When it came time to test, I prayed that my eyes would not stray. I prayed that I could read the letters and that they wouldn't blur together to say YOU CAN'T DO IT YOU CAN'T DO IT. My heart thumped a jillion miles a minute every time I took a test. But the fact is I passed.

●●

My first day at the Academy was an adventure, to say the least. I got orders to report to the Academy by 5 PM and to check in, receive my clothing, and my assigned bunk.

I met the supervisor at the facility and checked in. Boy, did I have reservations, not the ones at a hotel, either. The supervisor was dressed in green and khaki garb and had on a drill instructor's hat. The hat was called a Smoky the Bear Hat because it resembled the hat that Smoky the Bear wore as a Forest Ranger or as a drill instructor in the army might wear.

I met a few people throughout the day and made new friends. We met at the classroom at 5 pm. and that's where my life ended as I knew it.

The staff, then the Captain of the Academy, introduced us all and then gave us the mission statement. All of our concerns, our needs and our lives for the next two months would be at their beck and call.

That Smokey the Bear hat should have been a clue of what was to come. Our mornings began at 4:30 am and ended at 9 pm daily. What the hell was I doing here? My heart doesn't get started at 4:30 am and Monday was the beginning of hell week. Yelling, screaming instructors who hated people in general. Where's my damned truck? They'll never miss me. I'm in the wind....

A few of the class stayed on campus during the weekend and became fast friends. Some became fast friends with the instructors. Like I was trying to get into my car on a Friday evening and two of 'em making out like a coupla high school kids -- an instructor and one of the female cadets. I assume they were just doing that – I didn't check for details. I hightailed it out of there wondering about the comfort of their situation. Pretty tight looking to me....Not my cup of tea. Oh well, each to his own. But I thought, "I bet she'll pass!" She did.

There was classroom training all day, with lunch, then afternoon classroom training until 5 AM or so. Not to mention, evening work assignments. All eyes were on us as we ate, went to class, did physical raining etc. The hard part came with the stress of the Academy!!

There were people from different backgrounds, trying to become one. We attempted to learn to assist one another and to depend on one another, with moderate success. This was more than a team concept, because your life depended on how your peers would react in a situation. I never thought how I would depend on someone else to help me in a crisis, much less a riot.

Aerobics were foreign to me, as were pushups and sit-ups. I had to accelerate my physical fitness in order to do the job. "Cut out fast food? Walk faster and longer? No smoking?" Was I on the Oprah *Let's Change our Life* segment?

The physical part of the academy was different than training on my own. I had to do it with forty-some other people at their pace and not mine. It was hard at first, harder secondly, and hardest yet at the end!

Each morning I would fall out for physical training. I hated it. I hated it so much in the dark, the cold and mix that up with sweat. How bad can it get? Everyone kind of had a hard time acclimating to the rigor of enforced exercise.

Of course, there is always that one asshole. The one that loves to make everyone else feel horrible. He speeds around the track, does a flip or two, and smiles all the while. Meanwhile, I'm on ground zero, ready to launch off.

Some of the faster guys would slow their pace down, so the others of us wouldn't look so bad. Pretty nice of them, I guess. I don't know if I could do that. But it didn't make the few of us slow ones look so bad.

Self defense training was an oxymoron. First, you are sweating like a pig. You look like one, too and you gotta fall down on the mat and roll over and get right back up. Shit. Once I was down, I wanted to stay down. No kidding.

Would things get better? Could I pass this part of the training? I had my doubts. So did others.

Then once you were up, you had to grab an instructor and pull him to the mat without trying. Hooray for brawn! I was big. It was easy to grab some guy and pull him down on the mat.

You had to have keen eyes looking at all your surroundings. 'Cause those sonabitches would get together and try to sabotage you. I usually had great success in that arena. And it was kind of fun like when little boys play and shove each other. Yep, the testosterone stirred quite a bit then. Aggression was acceptable.

One female would grab an instructor and then this high-pitched screech would come from her mouth and all our eardrums were invaded.

She huffed and puffed just like that bad ole' wolf, but she couldn't bring him down. Later on she found out it wasn't brawn that did it, but leverage. If you know the tricks, you can do it.

The weight room was a killer. My friend could lift a house if he needed to. We did strength training — lighter weights, but more repetitions. I started with 60 pounds and went up from there. I never realized that getting into shape could be so hard.

Then they fucked up our driving by recreating rules of the road and those who don't follow them — we had

to learn to be defensive drivers and how to reshape
our attitudes. No longer was it automatic that our
middle digits would display themselves when
someone pulled around us too closely.

"Move, you jerk," you might mutter under your
breath, but on the outside, you had to look cool,
calm, and collected or the shit would hit the fan and
you were harassed some more until you could take it.

It's pretty hard dealing with angry, mean people and
just taking it with aplomb. Not a bomb, but savvy and
grace!

When Bill Murray and John Candy starred in Stripes,
you better bet all the cadets watched that flick with
extreme interest. They would tease me and call me
John Candy. Well, I did look like him and back then it
wasn't funny, but watching reruns it is hysterical.

Sometimes I felt that they needed to carry me off in
an ambulance, I was so tired. But if you wanted it
bad enough, they said, "No pain, No Gain." Bullshit.
But it was their store and they were the ones in
charge!

After PT came breakfast – yum, starch, starch, and more
starch. The mess hall cook wore whites, army boots and had a
U.S. Army insignia on his uniform. I observed his name, rank.
What rank?

This was not the military. Why was he wearing the insignia of
an E-7 Sergeant? I thought, what the hell, and as I

approached him, he growled at me! I asked him why he was wearing the insignia of an E-7 on his collars. Did he not know that he was in violation of the UCMJ (Uniform Code of Military Justice), by wearing that insignia? He looked at me and then like that he changed his tune and became more pleasant and less gruff.

Then he offered me steak and eggs for breakfast. I found out he was a cook in the Army and retired as such. At the noon meal (lunch), the insignia was gone and he was very pleasant to me for the rest of my training. Thus, this taught me to confront the workers to see the correct way things were to be done.

The Academy was interesting and the classroom exercises fun. We studied all together for the assigned tests and quizzes. The approach to the Academy was that we all worked together and if it was necessary, we had to help any of our struggling cadets as a team.

My first test wasn't as intimidating as I had perceived it might be. Most of the training consisted of classroom, physical, and weapon's training.

We had skits to be used for Confrontation Alley. This would have certain tasks assigned to us and to complete. As an example, we came into the television room and inmates, (played by the instructors), would have the television on excessively loud, and our job would be to have the TV's turned down without causing a riot!

Well, since I was one of the biggest people there, I was selected. I showed that I was firm, consistent, and conscientious.

Looking around the room, I saw someone with a smirk on his face. Yeah, that might be the troublemaker. I eyed him really good. I moved in closer. Closer yet, invading his space.

"You," I pointed to him. "You come with me."

At first he just glared at me. I glared back. It was good I was about 50 pounds heavier than he. He got up and I escorted him to another part of the room. Then I turned the damned TV down.

Another fun skit – well, it was fun for the instructors:

"Guard! Guard! Scuffling in the housing unit. Go quell the noise before someone gets hurt."

We were on our way. Click, clickety click. Our heels struck the cement floors as we quickly moved to the site of unrest.

As I approached the staged hiatus, I noticed two guys getting ready to rumble.

"You asshole!" shouted the bigger, robust guy.

"Damn it, butthead, I didn't touch your cigs," whined the other, slimmer version of a Pee Wee Herman.

The bigger one grabbed the smaller one in a chokehold. For a moment I was afraid this was the real thing gone wrong. Shit. Did I have backup? I looked behind me. Yeah. I looked at the guys scuffling.

"Break it up, now!" my voice boomed. Was that me speaking? The combatants looked up at me for a moment. I took advantage of that break and grabbed the bigger guy and swung his arms around his back.

"Ow, you're hurting me," he shouted pretty damned realistically. I wasn't sure if I was really hurting him or not, but, hell, they were the ones who started this play. I cuffed him and separated them. Whew.

You can't just play. You gotta write it all up. You gotta identify the aggressor, if possible, and then taking the inmates to the infirmary for first aid and then write a report. Sweat was pouring down my face as I huffed and puffed. This was hard work. This was man's work. Yeah.

"You know, Sieren seems to have a knack for working with violence and violent people," I overheard one of the instructors saying. Ha! Must have been my training at the Army Depot or maybe Pop's army demeanor at home. Tough, but inside he was a pussycat.

Our written tests were comprehensive and we needed to maintain a B average to stay in the Academy. I remember my second test. I forgot to turn the last page and both sides of the test were not completed, although I received a 75%, I needed 85% to continue.

"Hey, sir," I anguished inside. "Sir, lookie here."

The instructor realized that the pages stuck together.

"Hum," he pondered. "I do believe you need another chance to take this exam over." I wanted to hug and kiss him. Well, not really. But I was pretty damned happy that he had a heart. Would everyone care like that? Or be fair? Or even listen or look? I was allowed to retake the 2nd exam.

My friend, Anthony, helped me study and after the make-up test was administered, I had received 90%, however a 85% was the max I could receive. I was already ready to quit the Academy, but without my friend Anthony I would not have taken and passed the test. I also learned to write the four W's and one H. Who, what, were, when and how as a format in writing reports. I thought that the tests were easy, if you studied and remembered to answer the questions on the last page of the test!

I finished the tests and we were scheduled to take another critical part of the Academy. As we progressed to another exciting part of the Academy, this would show who was real and who was a faker.

Chapter 6
The Dreaded Gas Chamber

One of the worst things we had to endure was the gas chamber, not at San Quentin, but the one at the Training Academy. I remember, the company sergeants selected one of our cadets to be our company cadet, or CADET X.

As we were trucked to the area were the chamber was, we would all march into the chamber and then take off our gas masks, like in Army or Police training. What a mess, people were coughing, snot running down our face, eyes watering and our Cadet X, you thought he was dying carrying on and on.

Well, after the initial sensations wore off and we wiped our faces, Cadet X announces, "Let's do it again."

Oh, brother, what a geek, kiss ass and jerk!! He looked like Howdy Dowdy and bugged the shit out of all of us – he resembled the dummy, of course!! This was not the first time that the CADET X, would act as if he were top dog. As we returned to the Academy and got ready for inspection, Cadet X was acting as if he was the instructor and trying to ride us, well, that is another story; anyway, we rose the next morning at 4:30 am , ready for more PT.

I remember, "MORE PT" SERGEANT, "MORE PT". As we ran around the track in the middle of a cold wet morning, I decided to take a break.

So I stopped running, took out and lit my Salem and had a long smoke. This seemed to be the right thing to do; it was cold, wet, and I was tired of listening to this wannabe. Then

Eyes Within

Cadet X saw me taking a break and verbally and without provocation pushed me and yelled for me to continue the run.

I yelled, I'll break you in half, you scrawny son of a bitch!"

He yelled and took off. Then my friends held me back because I wanted to strangle the twerp. After that incident, he never came back to me, spoke or asked any questions of me. I guess being tough and big, and standing your ground is where it is at. After that incident, it was shower, shave, and, well, you know the rest.

Another day and another day closer to graduation. My gut told me to keep on going. The next exciting and dangerous phase of our training was going to the range. I did not know how dangerous that was! At the shooting range, we had to qualify with the pistol, rifle and the shotgun.

I scored average with the handgun and the rifle; however, I was deadly with the shotgun. It was so cold that one of the cadets forgot their gloves and wore socks, hence his nickname. We ate between times and it was always starch, starch, and more starch.

Weapons training on that kind of food was even scarier. Most of us could not hit the side of a barn. Socks continued using his socks because they grabbed better and allowed him to be steadier on the shot. I knew to duck when some of the guys were shooting. If you talked to them, they'd turn with their weapon aimed at you. Shit, this was dangerous enough and we're not trying to kill each other.

Eyes Within

Chapter 7
On the Job Training – Just in Time!

Even though the Academy was hard at times, I was lucky to meet a great bunch of people to work with. Most of the cadets had not shot any kind of weapons, it was obvious, and we almost shot ourselves. I sure hoped we wouldn't have to shoot a warning shot 'cut we might kill someone.

Three days on the job training, or OJT, was next, so we headed out for DVI, or Dual Vocational Institution. The prison cells (houses), as the inmates call them, were four ½ feet or so wide, by 6'4" tall and 5 to six 6 feet long.

Now this might seem large or if you each have 6 cubic feet of personal property, seem small for one average person, but for a large person, it was tiny. Well, if you can't do the time you shouldn't do the crime, as they say.

Searching cells and the yard one day, we followed the staff very closely. We wore brown rags making us look more like deliverymen than guards. We tried to act big like them and not be afraid of small places. I was given one cell to search and as I did, an inmate came galloping back from the dispensary, yelling, "What the hell are you doing?"

I guess I had that deer in the headlights look again, 'cause he softened a bit when I shakily answered, "I'm the UPS man." He guffawed and laughed so hard he almost split his side open.

He allowed me to complete the search and I gave him a list of the three contraband items I took and thanked him for his cooperation.

He laughed a low laugh and said, "Hey, kid, you're gonna make a fine cop." I sighed a sigh of complete relief and almost wanted to hug the guy. I left in a hurry

The yard was "locked down", and we all searched for several hours and found more Inmate manufactured weapons or "shanks." The facility was on alert and inmates were escorted in groups to dinner, i.e. "chow". The supervisor would point out inmates   that he selected at random to be searched i.e.; clothed body search.

"Yuck, they should take a bath before this is done," I murmured to myself. "Thank God I have my gloves on."

Back at the academy they stressed agility – both mental and physical and that surely helped when I got to the big place, 'cause those inmates got nothing better to do than sit and think of ways to fuck up your day.

Confrontation Alley was a simulation whereby academy trainees needed to understand what it might be like in the real prison. One time one instructor was yelling, "Cease, cease!"

I kept on running. He screamed again, "Cease, cease!" I finally stopped and looked at him quizzically. He asked me what the hell I thought I was doing. I replied, 'I have no idea what you are saying!" He laughed and repeated – "Cease means to stop!"

"Well, isn't that what I did?"

After dinner, we continued the search and then returned to the Academy.

The next day we returned to DVI and searched the cells, discarding excess state property and removed contraband items. Then we would log the information down in a logbook and give out mail before dinner.

This count presented some difficult times for some female and male cadets, etc. Some of the convicts like to call their messing around "beating the monkey" or "the sock of joy." The true word is masturbation. That can cause a problem for some innocent one just learning to be a guard. You are counting and, whoa, baby! What's happening' here?

The convicts didn't care who saw them. If they wanted to do it, they did it. No big deal. As a matter of fact, some of the hardened criminals especially got a kick out of people watching them, especially the women.

Well, be as it may, an inmate was completing his foray into happy land, as one of the female officers looked in to count him. She yelled at him and he laughed. The inmate was written up, but what the hell? He was a lifer, so what? He didn't care.

I found out quickly that most of the inmates don't care; they think that society made them and society owed them a decent life. I always was taught to treat people the way you wanted them to treat you, oh, boy, how wrong and right that statement was. Sometimes it depended on what the situation was and who was involved.

As we completed our OJT at DVI, we were told that Vacaville was our next stop on the next day so off to the Academy, 2 down and one more OJT to go. Oh, I guess I'll tell you about CADET X, and his rampage.

We returned to the Academy after our training at the GAS Range. I never forget the way he acted coughing and screaming as he ran out of the chamber. I thought what a sissy and a joke. He was brought to task and was formally dismissed as the company commander.

Cadet X soon after that incident became the X cadet. He made threats that he would come back and get us all. Nice guy, eh? The administration documented his behaviors thus protecting the staff and evidently the state and thus keeping him from reapplying later.

What a relief that he was gone. Jerk! OJT, here we come!!

Our next training would be at CMF, California Medical Facility, for our last OJT during training.

It was a cold morning when we arrived at CMF and the smell of rain permeated the air. It was fresh and cool and clean smelling. For a while the air in the prison was quiet and strangely stagnant.

"You see," one officer said, "an officer was stabbed early this morning. He's my friend," he ended with a stifled sob. All I wanted to know if the son of a bitch was dead. Shit – I then knew I was walking the toughest beat in prison!

I asked him what had gone down and he said that the inmates didn't like this officer so they kept telling another inmate that this officer had it in for him.

No one knew this was going to happen. That was the day I learned there is a mix of sociopaths, murderers, rapists, robbers and so on who certainly do not care about anything else but themselves! The fun of the day now was now the dread of the day.

The academy sergeant took us to our designated areas and we paired up with other correctional officers and went to different units in preparation for the
Day's events.

The whole area seemed so somber and surreal. Was murder commonplace in this hole?

The area we began was the he/she dorms. The reason for the he/she dorm is that some of the men looked like woman, really almost like women.

Well, some except for the faces with beards that sounded like and had female equipment. The sergeant told me to go over and have the inmate cutting in line to move back and as I approached her, I said, "Excuse me," then she turned around and from the chest down she appeared to be a she!

Well, from the voice, which was a gruff sounding one, to the hairy knuckles, I was completely confused.

Why was the state allowing these guys to look like this, dress and act like they were women? I soon found out that not only did they look like women, but they were allowed to act as if they were married to guys.

They didn't have a cell mate but a husband or wife!! I couldn't believe that this was like a city within four walls. Everyone just living as if this was a normal way of life.

Then just as I thought how weird and calm it was, an alarm sounded-- a red light blinked down the corridor!! An eerie sound, like at the entry to a foghorn or bay doors opening at the local lumberyard. I saw inmates standing against the walls and staff running towards me.

Well, I got a choice, either stand by a wall or run towards the light and foghorn. I ran towards the lights and foghorn. My heart was thumping so hard I thought it was going to pop out of my chest. As we arrived, the crowd split up revealing two inmates slapping each other.

Then I noticed, no, not slapping each other, but, slashing.

They were broken up and placed in handcuffs, then taken to the medical
department for checkups, then off to the sergeant's office. Since I was one of the first ones on the scene, I got into the action.
I spoke to the program sergeant, gave him my report of what happened and he thanked me for all my work and then offered me a slot when I was available. I was honored that I

hadn't even started work and already had some accolades. Or something like that.

Well, four more hours and back to the Academy.

Chapter 8
A Real Job

Finally, the big day, my background cleared, and the first offer was Soledad State Prison, too far, then San Quinton, no, still too far. Finally, CMF, during the last months. I wondered where in the hell CME was and I then found out it was in Vacaville CA. I then learned my date to report was later in the winter of 1984.

A level 3 prison always gets the rejects from other prisons. That worked at our new building as well. We got the child rapists, the worst of the bunch, and a lot of maniacal men who were ready to kill others, as well as themselves.

Even Charley Manson was there for a while. While others were a bit frightened of him because he had this friggin' stare that could see inside you. I wasn't afraid of him, 'cause I was twice his size for Christ's sake.

He'd bribe the guards and promise a good story for a pack of cigs. I never sat and prostituted myself to him for any ole' story. He was just like the others as far as I was concerned. He went to another prison and ruined the dreams of many an officer who thought they could write the true story of Charley. Shit, true story – he was a murderer, convicted, and serving his term. What story?

The men and women who wanted to be officers were a diverse group. Some wanted power and those were the ones who really didn't make it. Those were the ones who made little mistakes and became beholden to the inmates.

One little impropriety and boom! The inmate had ya. First, it is a request for cigarettes and then on to drugs and alcohol. Then the officer is compromised but good.

It always hurt when one of your own was behind bars. One little mistake and wham – they go from guard to inmate in no time. One officer started out feeling sorry for an inmate. That feeling encouraged friendship and that's where the guard made his mistake. First, one little act of impropriety – a gift – turned into more than just cigarettes. Running drugs. Which worked out fine for a while for the two of them until the guard got caught. Bam. On the inside. He treated the rest of the guards respectfully and fully recognized his mistake. Although he was an inmate for a while, he was a model inmate, ready to make restitution and go back to another life. For a guard – he would never be again.

I've never understood that kind of thinking. My parents raised me to be honest and hard working. How could this man jeopardize his family and self for a few hundred bucks? It ain't worth it, man, it ain't worth it.

The majority of the guards recognize that and are honest and forthright individuals. I was blessed to be among their ranks, I suppose.

Sexual harassment is rampant in the prisons some people think. Well, there was one little ole' gal who was getting overly friendly with the inmates and when her boyfriend found out (non-inmate), he exploded and she had to side-step his wrath and figure out a way to stay out of trouble.

She was also written up by staff as fraternizing with inmates, which is a punishable offense of losing your job. So she and her boyfriend concocted a story about some of the guards making overtures to her and sought some duped counselor to represent her.

Well, during this time I was out on sick leave and I didn't know what was coming down. Turns out this woman said that the guards were asking her out on dates and she even described them in detail. I was described as much smaller and with habits I did not ever have! Plus I was not even there – I was out sick.

The state spent lots of money supporting their employees to their credit and she got nothing and lost her job. But the expense and the sheer agony of being accused of something that you've never even thought of doing, much less done, is something that can never be erased from an individual's spirit. Wonder if it was worth it to her? I know I could never live with myself if I did someone dirty. That's just isn't in my psyche at all.

As far as someone being someone's bitch in the pen – that happens, but not as much as one might think. It certainly isn't paraded in front of the staff, but you know it happens by those who happen to tell you. You know when you see a fight break out because someone broke up. It might be funny, but it's too sad to laugh at.

It behooves a future prison employee to be big and strong. Weak, little people don't fare as well. My size invoked respect, if not my attitude of generosity, kindness, and justice.

I may have been all pumped up like a peacock, but deep down inside I am like Pop – a pussycat inside.

After moving from one prison to a promoted position at another prison, some of the inmates recognized me. "Hey, Sarge! How are you?" Others just stared in wonder.

"Hey, Sarge, there are some others here from X prison. Look 'em up!"

So I asked the guard to unlock this guy's cell, get me a soda, and I told the inmate named Mac that we could talk a bit. He brought me up on the latest and commented that this new place surely wasn't run as well as the last.

"Sarge, here they tell on each other. Staff tells on staff."

Administrators tell on administrators and all the convicts tell on each other."

I replied with a sigh, "Mac, I thought so. I sure appreciate talking with you."

I pat him on the back and returned him to his cell. For the duration of my time at that institution, Mac remained a dependable source of information I would otherwise not have garnered.
Years later, as my wife and I were walking down the street, I heard, "Hey, Sarge, hey, Sarge!"

I looked around and there was Mac, beaming. He was on the outside and had his arm around a burly, yet becoming lady.

"I want you to meet my wife, Nancy. Nancy, this is the best man I've ever met. He is a true gentleman and just as hell."

I smiled. It was nice to know that Mac was giving himself a chance to live a better life. From the looks of Nancy, I could tell she was a decent woman who just might help him make it.

I introduced my embarrassed wife and we made small talk and parted our ways. You never know whom you will meet walking down the street of life. That's the way of the guard, the sarge, the lieutenant, and the captain – you have to live your life as if in a mirror.

Everyone is watching you and what you do. If you do that, you won't regret it. But if for a moment you put down your guard and do something off task, illegal, or immoral, you will get caught. That's just the way it goes. Living by that advice has kept me on the straight and narrow.

Chapter Nine
Sanity?

Sometimes when I was on yard duty, my friend Hank would also be assigned to help. We would be checking for weapons in the ground. I don't mean just lying about – I mean UNDER the ground. The best place to find them was near the fence, 'cause the metal detectors would detect the fence and not the weapon.

On any given day we would find several hand-made weapons. We used to joke that we had found so many made from metal parts in the prison, that one day the whole thing would implode due to all the holes left by the stolen pieces.

We joked a lot and that suppressed the negative emotions that are just a normal part of working with the hard core of life. When you work with murderers who are not repentant and rapists who want to get out and do it again, it starts to get to you and you have to sieve out the negative and focus in on the positive.

I would say that 99% of the felons incarcerated will do it again and most return to the pen.

Hank turned out to be a great guy! Good enough to marry my sister, indeed. Hank would laugh at everything. Everyone liked him – you couldn't help it. Sometimes he would laugh at his own jokes so hard you could hardly understand what he was laughing at.

"Booyah!" he'd shout. "Comin' in. Help me, help me! I've fallen and can't get up."

Eyes Within

The inmates would laugh and sometimes even applaud his comic antics. He believed in treating everyone with respect and that is what kept him doing what he did and doing it well. Everyone knows that humor is preventative medicine. Hank used it well.

One night on graveyard shift, I was working overtime in Building 2 and Hank was in Building 5. We heard a Code 3 going off over the radio and we both ran like leopards on the chase to Building 4 where assistance was needed. Running through the dark, rainy mud, both of us slipped. I brushed myself off and ran in to Building 4. Hank was following huffing and puffing and cold as a snake in its lair.

"What's up?" we chorused.

"MOUSE." Loud and clear.

Hank looked at me. I looked at Hank. Mouse? Was that a new code word or what? Mouse?

"MOUSE." The officer reiterated.

He began to move toward a cell and we cautiously followed. Inside an inmate was hollering and shrieking and jumping all over.

Mouse. We got it. There was a damned mouse in the cell. We opened the cell, calmed down the inmate and took a broom to rid the cell of the rodent.

We searched all over for any other evidence of a MOUSE. Yes, mouse. None. But the inmate did not want to return to his cell. He was scared to death. Evidently not only had this little mouse invaded the inmate's house, but he had scurried across his chest as well and woke him up. No sir. He was not going to go back in that cell.

I pondered the situation and we went back, swept wildly, pulled up sheets and shook them out. No MOUSE. No, no mouse in this house.

I showed him around and told him he could put a towel under his door in order to keep any future visitors of the small furry kind out of his room. He thanked us and calmed down. That was one weird code call.

When Hank had to take the inmates out for fresh air, he would chirp merrily, "Let's follow the leader!" Then that damned lovable fool would start a Pied Piper sort of line and the inmates would look at each other, at me, and follow, with some even dancing like Hank. Smiling and out in the sun were formulas for peace – for a while anyway.
Sometimes out in the yard the fellas would have had time to concoct fights in advance. Much like my first day, but these days I was no rookie and knew what to do and how to do it. Maybe someone was shorted some drugs or maybe someone was someone else's new boyfriend. Who knows? But boredom and time on your hands makes the man mighty jumpy.

Mac even let me know when a fight was schedule to erupt – told me I should call in sick the next day and not get hurt. Of course, I thanked him for the advice, but had to go straight to the lieutenant and inform him. Naturally, I came the next day and no fight ensued. Some guards might have seen that as a great opportunity to save their skins. I guess I wasn't thinking of my skin at the time.

We knew that one moment might seem idyllic and the next all hell would break out. Usually a yard fight meant everyone had to be detained, pulled apart, and sent back inside. The adrenaline rush was what made it possible for us to handle this. And no fear. If you were afraid, they could smell it in you. Everyone knew that I was not afraid. If I ever was, they would never smell it on me. I could stare down the meanest son of a bitch.

Hank and I became best friends. We'd march the inmates military style and got a kick out of saying, "Left, right, left, right!" The inmates got in line and marched, by God.

Sometimes it seemed we were two little boys playing games. But some inmates actually needed that sort of routine and regiment. We gladly provided it for them.

When an inmate was discharged gone out the door, Hank would say goodbye, "Now, ya'll come back, ya hear? And bring a friend with ya."

Sadly, a lot did come back. We had some father and son combos in cells and then some odd combinations.

One day while I was taking count – we counted those suckers day and night – several times. We had to make sure they were alive.

So, as I peeked into this one cell, I saw an inmate half naked getting ready to pleasure himself with another inmate. I got to admit I was embarrassed somewhat and the watch captain asked me what I was gonna put down on the roster – they were both there – what was their activity?

Uh, well, let me see, the one had penis erectus. I couldn't bring myself to say he had a hard on. Don't know why that seemed too personal and something I shouldn't have had to observe.

It got around to the inmates and convicts and gave everyone a pretty good laugh. Erectus, indeed.

The difference between a convict and an inmate is usually age – a convict is there for the long haul and knows the rules and has made the prison his world. An inmate is usually someone new to the prison who doesn't know the routine or doesn't display adequate respect. The convicts fare much better than the inmates.

The convicts know what they have coming and they demand it. Once during a lockdown, Hank and I ended up in the kitchen. Now, I threw a little bit of this and a little bit of that in the stew or whatever that slop was.

The inmates were pretty unhappy. When the all clear came through, I'm not sure but that it wasn't my style of cooking that urged everyone to be cooperative. Now, if Hank had been cookin' – they'd a wanted to keep him there- he could cook some fine Italian dishes.

Chapter 10
It Ain't the Movies and Jesus Loves You

There are one man and two men cells usually in the prison and each one in California, that is, has a television, a cot with a good mattress, a toilet, and inmate's personal belongings.

It isn't like in the movies where they have numbered shirts and they are black and white striped, with big black balls and chains attached at their feet.

Their houses or cells are 8 feet x 8 feet x 6 feet. They are not large rooms, but the inmates have them stashed with personal items that have to be looked through whenever we are doing a search, which could be anytime they aren't expecting it. What are we looking for?

Well, contraband, either brought in by visitors or amply bestowed by the institution employees.

When family or friends come a visitin', we can search their outers, but we don't do internal searches. You'd be surprised at the number of contraband brought in through bodily orifices. One time a baby was crying and crying and the mother just shushed it and kept on looking ahead. I asked a female guard to check the child and there was a baggie of drugs in the child's diapers. No wonder that child was squirming and crying.

The "visitor" soon became inmate and the child a ward of the state. For what? Some cheap high or some money to buy a cigarette? A moment of pleasure for a lifetime of misery....

Yes, men in prison find Jesus. Jesus works for them and gets them out on parole. When they are out, Jesus disappears usually and they have to return to the pen for some more old-fashioned religion.

They get smarter and harder to catch the second time around. Others just resign themselves to the fact that the prison is better than outdoors. Here they are warm, have three meals a day, a private room, and an ability to learn, work out, enjoy free medical care, and entertain themselves. Some people never grow out of the need to be taken care of....

Food – that's always an interesting topic. Some of us guards and sergeants were taste-testers to taste the quality of food. One guard was a weight lifter. He'd take triple the food the others had. We told him he had to take what the inmates got!

Sometimes the servers would give extra portions to their friends and we had to watch to make sure that the 200 some men had equal portions. One officer watched the serving line and another made sure they stood with their shirts tucked in and stood orderly.

Another officer watched as the inmates sat. Eating time was a good time for disruptions. Inmate crews cleaned up and they got to eat leftovers, just as the cooks did. They all tried to follow the "man's rules." Hot meal for breakfast and dinner and sack lunch.

In the weight room we had an inmate to stack the weights. We had to count them and make sure they were all there. They were heavy as hell and if one disappeared, it could become an immediate weapon. How long did they use the weight room? Who used the weight room?

Any accidents in the weight room?

Speaking of accidents....One ole' guy who was a convict and probably would live out his life in the pen had a job as a laundry porter. He loved that job and whistled while he worked.

One day we had a Code 3 which meant that all inmates had to freeze and crouch down so the guards and administration could take a head count and find out what was going on.

Everyone got down, but Mikey. He kept going round the track picking up dirty linens. I ran to him and exclaimed, "Mikey, do you hear me? Did you hear the code?"

"Wall, ah thought it didn't mean me. I am an employee. I got this job.," he said as he proudly pointed to his hamper.

"No, no!" I quickly reiterated."You are still a convict – an inmate, ya understand? You gotta follow the rules for those guys. If you didn't, you might have gotten tackled or worse yet...."

His sunken eyes and demeanor lit up. He said quickly, "Oh, I gets it. I will do that the next time, buh-leave me!"

I knew he would. He was a pretty nice fella – one that could have used better parenting and upbringing and he would have made a model citizen. That's the kind that sort of breaks your heart.

Another time and another code, three of us went running like hell to where some help was needed. Now we had a new warden and she liked the place to look real pretty like.

We had daffodils and other flowers bloomin' everywhere. The maintenance guys were always cleaning. This particular day someone had just waxed the floors as my lieutenant, myself, and another sergeant ran to meet the emergency presenting itself.

Well, we unexpectedly created our own little emergency – as we rounded the corner, we all slipped on the wax and fell hard. I hit my head and eye. My lieutenant knocked himself out on the iron railing on the stairs and the other guy – hell, I don't even remember what happened to him.

Needless to say, I never found out what the other code had been for, since two of us ended up in the dispensary getting emergency first aid. The lieutenant was out for a few weeks, but I came back the next day. It got around that Sieren was some crazy son of a bitch. Leave him alone – that boy don't know pain when he sees it.

Well, not only was my head aching like hell, but my shoulder felt like a thousand prickly pears were invading it and trying to get out. That doesn't make for a fun day at the job. I ended up going to a specialist who said I needed surgery, so this crazy son of a bitch used a little sense and had that taken care of.

Back to that warden – even though everything looked good, most things mechanical did not work. Toilets wouldn't flush all the way. Doors needed new locks, but her idea was that if it looked nice, it must be working. Pissed quite a few of the staff off. What could we do about it?

Falling is just one of the risks of working in a high-risk, high-maintenance facility. When a code comes over the waves, you gotta go and you gotta run like the wind.

One time I ran out the door and onto the muddy yard and skidded and fell down. From up in the tower, I heard a smart-ass voice shout, "SAFE!" Yeah, that was good for a laugh or two. I was late for the emergency, whatever it was.

Chapter 11
Cooperation or death

Next to one of the prisons in which I worked was a juvenile facility and sometimes we traded little ole' shit prisoners. Man, those little punks are sometimes worse than the older guys.

They have no fear and think their shit don't stink. Well, some of them, that is. Others are scared shitless and, hopefully, that will be good for them, so they don't ever come back.

Well, back to the juvenile facility. One day we got a call to render some assistance. Seems that one of the Mexican kids supposedly had his daddy way down in Mexico sending a helicopter to rescue his son from the pen. I didn't believe it. It didn't happen, but it sure made for a lot of commotion for a while.

The city cops worked with us and we reciprocated in kind. For instance, if someone was stopped outside our facility, one of us would back up the city cop.

One particular funny guy loved coming up to the gate and shining his lights on the yard. He didn't think it was too funny when one of the guys shone the searchlight onto him! Our light was bigger than his. We laughed about that for a few days. Laughter helped us get through the bad times.

One young soldier turned into our facility and thought it was the base. He smelled to high heaven and we called the locals to come pick him up. They just called the base and the military came to claim their own. Poor guy – at first he thought it was a big shopping mall and then thought maybe it was the base. Drunk as a skunk!

Eyes Within

Funny thing is that most of us liked working in the prison. We didn't want to leave and the inmates couldn't wait until they left. Of course, the convicts knew better. The convicts were there for the long haul.

Eyes Within

Chapter 12
Some Things are Funny and Some aren't.....

Joking around together with the inmates allowed for an air of serenity to permeate the environment. Tension usually came when the guys couldn't go outside to vent their emotions.

Stuck inside 24/7 made for angry inmates and jumpy employees. Going outside in the sunshine, working out, gardening – all that helped their psyches.

 And even the psychos had psyches that could be helped. Even some of us were a little psycho.

Hank would start scratching himself like a dog. The inmates would say, "Hey, man, what's the matter?"

He'd reply, "Got the fugadugadoo."

"The what?"

"The fugadugadoo."

"Nah, you're kidding," they'd say hopefully.
"I got it and you better watch out that you don't get it," continued Hank scratching now like a maniac.

He'd move closer to the inmates and they'd cower in the corner. Then he'd say, "Whew. That was close – they must've jumped to you boys."

Then the scratching would begin and then someone would shout out, "You bastard! You are just kidding us! And I was dumb-assed enough to believe you."

But the funny thing is that we all felt like scratching, even knowing Hank was pulling our leg.

It was okay to laugh with the inmates, but being overly friendly was a definite negative. Some people just didn't get it. I sort of feel sorry for the women who fell into the tangled webs of the unloved and forlorn inmates.

One guy wrote the same letter to over a dozen women. All started out with, "Hey, baby. You know I love you. I can't wait to be with you. Uh, did you remember to deposit money in my account so I can buy the bare necessities here? If it weren't for you, I'd go crazy...."

We had the right to investigate mail as it came and went just to make sure contraband wasn't being sent back and forth. We all knew this guy was using these women.

Of course, we thought the women had to be losers, too. But that wasn't the point. At one point some of us discussed switching the letters, so that the women would get a clue. We didn't do it, but it was an enticing idea for sure.

I sat down with Tim one day and asked him why he did it. "Aren't you afraid that they will all find out about you?"

"Shit no. Those bitches have nothing better to do and if they do find out, I'll just find me some other bitches to support me."
Nice guy. Wonder what his mama would think of him? Damn. I'm pretty hard sounding, but I would never in my life take advantage of anyone. I wish I knew how to help this fucker.

That's just what he is. And women fall for him. He had ten years left to go so I guess he just needed to feel powerful.

I guess he's one of them who hadn't found Jesus yet. You know they all do – well, most of them, until they get out. A small percentage really do find God, but the others use it as a ruse to get early probation or parole. Jesus do his job mighty fine in the pen.

We had one guy a preachin' about hell and firestone and when he got out, he became known as the ATM bandit. The son of a bitch killed over a dozen people.

The way the authorities found out about it is that his last victim didn't die after being shot and thrown down a rocky, muddy ravine. He identified the ATM bandit and back came the convict home to the pen.

What people don't understand about the criminal mind is that the majority of convicts, inmates, or what have you, will re-offend given the choice. They are not nice people. They haven't been raised with good morals. They didn't have good role models, so how can all these goody two-shoes come trottin' in thinking they can rehabilitate some crazy bastard?

Our job was just to keep the peace, help them complete their sentence without becoming even more insane, and prepare for re-entry into society.

We tried to order pizza or hamburgers once in a while, so they wouldn't become so removed from society that they would really freak out when they did get out. If they did ever get out.

Chapter 13
Fraternization

The majority of the staff treated the inmates with respect. Sometimes with too much love. Rarely with disrespect. If you became "friends" with one of them, they could use that against you. Tell on you, ask for special privileges, etc. I reminded them when they wanted to go have coffee with me or meet me and my wife --

"I'm sorry, but the rule here is that I can't fraternize with you. I love my job and I respect you, but I can't bend the rules. Please understand." That usually worked well.

Now if I had met a few of these guys on the outside, I would have definitely become friends with them. One was an accountant and could help me work on my count faster than me sitting there ploddin' and wastin' time.

He enjoyed helping and never asked for any help. He is one I think will be successful when he gets out.

Some of the female guards fraternized with the inmates. One was a lonely divorcee who was pretty damned good looking and she brought a Polaroid picture of herself butt-naked to give to her lover. Well, she probably wouldn't have been found out, but we do surprise searches and one of the guards found the picture and identified it as an employee and told on her.

She was fired, but went to the union, and, surprisingly, she was reinstated with her job. That shocked me. Damn. But she was one of the lucky ones. One male guard fell in love with a he/she as we called them.

This he/she was beautiful and you could not tell for a moment that he was a she or vice versa. Well, this guard was getting a good blowjob when he was caught. When he found out that he was having a "love affair" with a he/she, he almost died. I can't imagine what it was like telling his wife....He lost his job and was not reinstated.

Working at the state prison or any prison is a very serious job. That doesn't mean you can't enjoy it, but you have to use your fuckin' head. If you don't, then you won't make it. Keeping your personal life at home is the best advice anyone ever gave me. If I had brought that to work, I'd probably have punched someone and ended up in a cell by myself.

Eyes Within

Chapter 14
Types of Inmates

Most convicts, inmates, yeah, criminals, belong in the pen if that is where they are. It might be that they haven't had a good upbringing, but they sure as hell are 99.9% guilty.

If you get one in a good mood and he's a thinkin' others are listenin', he might even brag about his crimes. On the other hand, on Sunday he will sob and cry to Jesus how sorry he is. Yeah, he's sorry he got caught that's what.

These ole' boys got all day to watch us and to watch us close. They know our weaknesses. One ole' guy kept telling me how cute I was.

Now I was 6'4" and weighed about 275 (nah, I always lie about my height and weight – I was probably 6'5" and 300 lbs.

Anyways, this ole' guy kept complimenting me and it felt damned funny. I didn't even like the way it felt. So I thought I would make myself ugly. I grew a mustache and gained about 50 more pounds. That damned idiot still thought I was cute. I made sure I never checked his cell alone! He knew my weakness. He thought I might be homophobic. Well, hell, I guess I was. I sure as hell didn't want to be anyone's bitch. I wasn't even my own wife's bitch!

Women guards had it particularly difficult, especially if they were newly divorced or getting over some love affair. Now, all of these guys in the pen clean up pretty nice. They gotta go to chow looking spiffy. Gotta have pants and shoes on with a shirt that 's tucked in.

They don't have to have short hair, but why the hell have long hair? Lots easier to just sprints and go. They had time to bulk up and get strong.

On the other hand, we were sleep-deprived and living off greasy cheeseburgers and fries. Oh, and about a dozen cokes per shift. When I worked more than one shift in a row, I ended up high on coke and I'm talkin' coca cola!
So when it came to emergencies, it was no wonder it was a struggle for the guards to protect themselves and keep the inmates down. We had to rely on our wits rather than our brawn. If we didn't, they'd get us every time.

Those damn bastards made weapons out of everything conceivable. I had to check the yard regularly to find shards of metal that could be used for knives. They started getting smarter than us.

At first we thought we had outsmarted them by finding the metal weapons near the fence. But then they were one up on us by manufacturing lethal weapons out of plastic. You see, they had nothing else to do, especially the lifers. It was a game for them.

Not for us. We were sometimes scared shitless. We would be sitting bullshitting and all of a sudden a code would ring and we would have to respond. Burp! The last bit of fries stuck in our throats and we were off like the Three Stooges. The majority of employee accidents were when we were running to assist. We would fall, slip, trip, and run out of wind.

The inmates were watching. They were there. The silent eyes saw what we did and could not do. It was like the enemy was lying in wait. Sometimes the game of hunt and hare was fun for us, too. Men are normally hunters and gatherers.

I wouldn't go so far as to say I would hunt down a man and kill him. That isn't my cup of tea. Shit, I can't even hurt a damned mole. I had one I almost named – that son of a bitch made about a bazillion holes in my yard, but I couldn't kill him. I could cuss him out real good, but to touch him or kill him – nah. That'd turn my stomach.

But some of these good ole' boys in the pen had already killed so many people, it didn't matter if one of us went down. It was the lure of the chase that excited them, I think.

But the gals – they were a different breed. They were nurturers. They felt sorry for the guys and fell for their stories more times than not. I'm not saying there aren't good women guards in the prison, but what I am saying is that more of them fell for the stories than did the guys. And that's what got them in trouble.

Why one ole' gal was kind of cute (even I thought so but would never ever say anything out loud) and she started bringing her boyfriend in his cell some dope. He demanded more and she even went to make a pick-up in her damned uniform. She was fired. Talked to the union. And got her damned job back.

That beat everything all to hell. How she did that I will never know. Was she trying to convince the prison she was trying to find out who else was doing drugs? Who knows. Strange things happen in the pen behind the bars and in front of them.

Like I said before, the inmates got a lot of time to look at and study the guards. They've got nothing better to do. The more intimate they become with their caretakers, the higher the chances are that they can bust out, or at least, have a lot more privileges than the rest of the inmates.

Chapter 15
Overtime and Food

We were always shorthanded. If it wasn't someone sick, someone caught in the middle of a yard fight, or someone attacked, it was someone who quit or was locked out for doing illegal and unethical things, such as bringing in contraband.

But another factor was soon realized – if you have no one to relieve you, you can't just walk on out after your shift. You gotta stay until relieved. That way many of us had 24 or 48-hour days. Then when you get off, it's mighty hard driving home.

Some of us drove more than an hour to work, so driving in the wee hours of the mornin' was amenable to big wrecks and sometimes deadly ones. It was always sad hearing about someone killed in an auto wreck on the way to or from work and it was more common that one might think.

A coupla times I almost fell asleep driving and then decided I wouldn't be a fool – I kind of like myself – so I stayed at a nearby hotel so I could be fresh the next morning and not compete with all the traffic jams and stress of driving a long distance.

We were also asked to volunteer for overtime – it was good money, but we earned every damned cent of it. It took us away from our families, made our inner timetables go topsy-turvy and in the end, the extra money wasn't worth it. But we all did it because most of us actually loved our jobs.

I mean we actually liked the fact that we could make a difference. If we made the convicts feel like people, they would relax and there wouldn't be a lot of problems in the yard. If we bellowed and swore at them and add to that a lot of heat in the hot California sun, well, you got a little bit of chaos a brewin'.

And another good thing about overtime was the cooks would cook us up some good grub, knowing that we didn't have time to go home and "make" lunch, etc. They always hated to strike or not do their job – we were just no match for their culinary skills. Whenever we had to cook (like if the kitchen staff got really pissed off and "struck," well, we either overcooked, undercooked, or certainly didn't season appropriately. Pretty soon, they'd come back grumbling that it wasn't worth that kind of shit.

When the sun got particularly blazing hot and the inmates started rumbling, we sometimes had barbecues. That was a bone of contention for all the staff. Some thought it was "coddling" the inmates and others saw it as a necessary redemption before the slaughter.

If we calmed these ole' boys down, then maybe, just maybe, they'd cool off and not fight, or at least, not fight as much. We were always looking out for them and for ourselves. You never knew from one minute to the other if this was gonna be your last breath on this dear ole' earth.

Eyes Within

Chapter 16
Going off the Deep End

The screams grew louder and louder. A code 3 was sounded. We ran out into the yard and couldn't see anyone on the ground, but the sounds grew louder and louder. We looked up and thought, "Holy shit!" There was the tower watch guy, holding his rifle, screaming, "Rats, rats, oh, God, get them off me!"

Someone, and I don't know who or how, got to him and replaced the rifle with a strong-arm. The ambulance was called and we later found out that the stupid son of a bitch was doing drugs and having hallucinations.

Now, what if he had started blasting with his rifle that he wasn't even supposed to be holding? Every time we touched any kind of firearm, we had to write a report as to why we had it in our possession.

Stupid, stupid, stupid son of a bitch. Ruined his life and his family's, as well as royally scared the bejeesus out of all of us. That was more common than not. Someone just losing his mind because of all the pressure and violence we had to witness and sometimes become part of....

Chapter 17
Once a Dog, Always a Dog

One of the funniest and probably, the most sadistic things I used in the penitentiary was to play the inmates at their own game! Well, they played us, so I thought If you can't beat join them... So when wakeup for chow was called,

I transformed my voice to that of a drug, barking dog.

Early in the morning I would accidentally, on purpose, open and close the Sally Port fast and keying the Mick. (MICROPHONE). This would sound like a dog coming into the housing unit. I would bark and growl and soon you would here several toilets flush throughout the cellblock. Then almost on key, I would return to the floor position and (as the Floor Officer), open a cell door, empty of course, and yell OK "CELL SEARCH", or in the movies they always say, ("SHAKE DOWN").

Of course, the inmates were too busy trying to get their drugs and other Contraband flushed or disposed of so they couldn't get busted. Sometimes I would key the mike and say, "Quack, Quack."

I did this for two reasons, first to catch the inmates who had contraband, and to have a little fun and really to relax tension in the housing unit. Also, this was to show the inmates that they were being gamed themselves.

Mostly the inmates never figured that the big dog was me.

I would hear about my shenanigan from my Program Sergeant, but hell it worked, and more drugs down the preferable tubes, and off the yard. I would laugh and thought, only if they knew. I thought it was funny, well, it worked and the drugs were being flushed down the toilet! Well, the "big shots" were looking for busts. I wasn't told how to get results but I did get them.

Eyes Within

Chapter 18
Lockdown

Other things come to mind during my time as an Officer. Some were funny and some were not. Things like when the yard was locked down, we in turn would have to feed the inmates hot breakfast, sacked lunches and hot dinners. Well. Since the inmate workers were on strike too, the Officers would have to fill in... Oh brother, what a mess.

The Staff would gather in the chow hall and we were the cooks, baggers, and place the food into the trays, throwaways and take the food to housing units and feed the inmates in their cells.

You can imagine how things turned out. The oatmeal and eggs were mixed up on the plate with the bacon that was either not real done, or bacon bits. Moreover, the potatoes were supposed to be hash browns; however, they turned to be black hash browns!

The juice was in a carton and it was placed into the styrofoam box and somehow leaked on the food.

Or, you might say tousled up onto the tray. You guessed it, what a mess! When the inmates opened the trays, we said, "Hay, nobody said we were perfect! Well, after a few days the inmate cooks decided not to be on strike any more.

The food was prepared well and all the complaints subsided. As we were professionals, we were trying to make these trays as good as the inmate workers. However, the staff and I simply didn't connect on this type of work. Most of us didn't even make eggs correctly, scrambled with a little of shell,

Oh well. I always said I could be a better ASS HOLE then the inmates could be.

Besides it wasn't like we planned it that way; it just happened. So we wouldn't
get an, A in Home Economics. I guess they think more clearly about a Strike in the future.....

Some of the inmates would come to work and make more messes than we did. I saw more than on one occasions meat fall off a tray and put back on. I was told when I questioned the inmate cook and he said,

"Well, it's only dirt and the cooking will cook it off".

Eyes Within

Chapter 19
Physical and Verbal Abuse

As staff, we were suppose to take some abuse, however, sometimes it became
unreal what inmates could think of what to call you. It would make the hair on
your neck crawl. We were told, hey, they're locked up for 5, 10 20 years to life so,
you have to learn to not be intimated into making mistakes... I always thought,"but what is good for the goose is good for the gander."

I never, I repeat, never intimated any verbal abuse, however, I would respond in
a snotty way, in order to show them I could get on their level.

For example, one inmate said, "I was with your wife last night, and she sure was a good fuck."

I nonchalantly turned to him and said, "I'm not married and your girl says hi, and that I am pretty refreshing after someone like you!"

As the stunned inmate got red in the face, I smiled and said, "You can dish it out, but can't take it, huh?"

Usually their homeboys would laugh and rip the guy some more. Believe me, this gave me credit in the respect aisle and showed that crude talk couldn't affect me. However, I didn't allow inmates to put their hands on me....

That's a simple philosophy. If they had, I am sure I would lose it. I was known as someone who wouldn't take any *crap* from anyone.

During my ten-year tenure, I had a lot of physical contacts, but I wasn't the one who
initiated the physical altercation. I was either breaking up a fight or I was in the
middle of a fight trying to break up the action. I always prided myself in the fact I was never the instigator; however, I could be the finisher.

I remember I was escorting this inmate from the housing unit and being dark he said,

"You know, I could jump you and no one will be able to save your ass!!!

I calmly said, "Well, all I have to do is fall down and the Tower Officer will shoot you, BANG, BANG."

I added that my mike was keyed and the inmate looked at my hand on the mike and
freaked as I smiled in a continuous and crazy fashion.

His frightened reply was, "No, don't do that!"

Every time I saw that inmate afterwards, I would say, "Hey, I feel drowsy," and he would glance nervously around and say, "Hey, Man, you're not right."

Eyes Within

Chapter 20
Cons are Always Cons

I remember when I would see inmates talking to their lawyers, especially the
young ones and the women. The inmate would lay it on so thick you could cut it
with a knife. The shit hit the fan. I mean it was so outrageous that anyone with an ounce of brains would realize that the inmate was lying through his teeth.

Usually the female lawyers would bring snacks and soft drinks to the inmate including cigarettes. This was a big NO, NO.

One day a suited female attorney was blatantly passing several packs of cigarettes to the inmate. As I approached, she glanced at me and I politely told her that she should know that we aren't allowed to give gifts to the inmates.

The inmate nervously dropped the can and spilled his drink. I asked him to clean up his mess, to which he replied as he plaintively looked at the attorney, "See what they make us do?"

Not quite believing what I had just heard, I asked the inmate right out, "Well, do you want me to clean up your mess?"

And, I'll be damned if that ole' woman attorney didn't just stand there, looking at me and said, "Well, you could help him."

Astonishment. This is how Inmates play their games and usually gain the confidence
of their victim and have other types of illegal activities occur at the victim's expense.

Convicts like to game their prey. They have a lot of time and a place in which to do their mischief. They can study you and wait. Sometimes staff lost their integrity, friends, and their job simply by getting caught up in the mesh of game playing.

Convicts will say anything to achieve a goal, whether it is to please someone, get favors gain your sympathy, or to have someone, or a group feel sorry for them.

Each day a convict thinks, "Hum, how can I play the system?" Once a convict "Goes Fishing", they usually say, "Look what they have done to me," or "Society has created us, we will parole one day," and, the one I like the best, "I have found the Lord Jesus Christ." I did not know he was lost!!! I learned and was taught several small things in life.

1. Take responsibility for your actions,

2. Don't blame others about your problems or misfortunes,

3. Correct any deficiencies,

4. Hard work won't kill you,

5. Treat people the way you want to be treated,

6. Don't take advantage of people,

7. Don't let people take advantage of you,

8.   Be kind not mean,

9.   Be honest and forthright,

10.   Earn your keep.....

These statements are what I think and what I continually remind myself to live by. Usually most convicts don't abide by them. I guess the Ten Commandments don't mean much to them either.

Their "Code of Ethics", are either, none or only a few of the ones listed above. I always observed convicts take advantage of the system, bleed and abuse the system. In general, abuse the system to their own advantage at other expense.

Let's take Number 1. Very few take responsibility for their actions. They are in Prison because of their bad life or the way they were raised. *No father or mother, no sister, no brother, no dog, no cat, etc. It's my fault, your fault,*

Society's fault but, never theirs. Oh, not all convicts verbalize these statements, but most of the ones I met in Prison did.

My lawyer was stupid, the judge was after me, the jury was prejudicial and this one is one of my favorite: The evidence was planted!

Every conceivable excuse was used to gain favor with anyone. What would this do you ask? Well, if a sympathetic person would fall into this trap, favors could be gained as a way of feeling sorry for the convict. As one person said to me,

"It all happened so fast. One minute I was listening to the inmate and then I felt myself feeling sorry for the inmate. Then, you guessed it, the inmate conned me to bring Contraband in to the Institution."

I didn't feel sorry for my colleague's poor choice. It was easy to be swayed by the cons, but we were trained professionals and should have known better. But sometimes we all decide to take the easy road.

Most inmates are the same, blaming others. They played on kindness and interpreted such as weakness.

Chapter 21
It's Over When The Fat Lady Sings or When You Get Hurt, Whichever Happens first

Eyes Within

You know, sometimes when you are right in the middle of a mess or situation, you don't appreciate it.

You complain about the hours, the hot water, or the way your boss looks at you. You feel sorry for yourself because you gotta drive 70 miles each way to work.

And one day it's all gone. Then you begin to see the silk on the sow's skin. Or something akin to that....

After it's gone, it's gone. And for all the melodrama, I know I miss the life of working in the penitentiary so much. As I sit here with my left leg possibly having to be removed, I wish I could return to that time.

The time of being with those who you counted on and those who covered your back. A time of camaraderie and of helping some just a little bit – maybe not a lot, but helping make others in this world feel that they aren't just some piece of shit, but that they are human and are deserving to be treated as humans.

I know a lot of people talk about life as it if it is nothing. Some of the hard-core guys did the very same. But it still was exhilarating at times to converse with them and talk about what life is all about. What happens when it 's gone? Where do we go? Do we have souls? Or is this just it?

When you get a bunch of men talking to the beat of drums like that you get some pretty intense things coming out. That's what I'm missing now. I sit day after day in my nice Southern California home with myself for company all day.

Eyes Within

The wife goes and comes but I'm still there 24/7. It's like my own little prison, but if I want I can still leave it. It's just too much trouble. The cast is heavy on my leg.

The painkillers are beginning to outlive their usefulness. Even the doctor is pessimistic. I've no children to visit me and the nearest blood relative is 500 miles away.

Regrets working in the pen? None whatsoever. Regrets having to retire? All in the world, but there is nothing I can do to change that.

Additional Note: In November, 2006, I did have my leg amputated – this certainly chronicled the end of any possible career in the penitentiary being restarted.

Now I am on my own journey, learning how to live with a useless prosthetic that hurts and doesn't even fit and learning to be independent. A long shot from a barking dog and a sergeant who cared for others....

www.ingramcontent.com/pod-product-compliance
Lightning Source LLC
Chambersburg PA
CBHW072318290526
45794CB00002B/705